STEM Careers

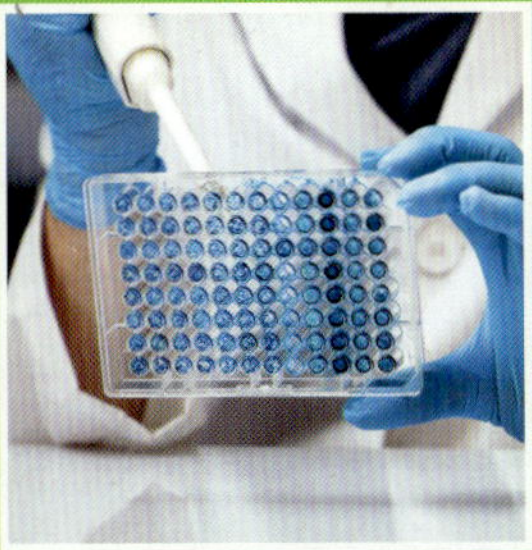

BIOLOGIST

Joy Gregory

AV2
www.av2books.com

Step 1
Go to **www.av2books.com**

Step 2
Enter this unique code
MYRDXXIS4

Step 3
Explore your interactive eBook!

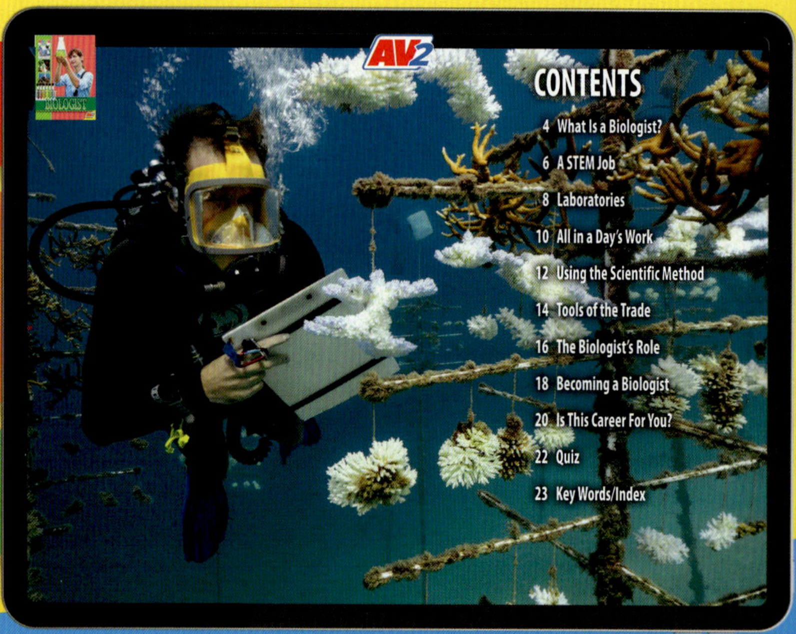

AV2 is optimized for use on any device

Your interactive eBook comes with...

Contents
Browse a live contents page to easily navigate through resources

Audio
Listen to sections of the book read aloud

Videos
Watch informative video clips

Weblinks
Gain additional information for research

Try This!
Complete activities and hands-on experiments

Key Words
Study vocabulary, and complete a matching word activity

Quizzes
Test your knowledge

Slideshows
View images and captions

... and much, much more!

BIOLOGIST

Contents

What Is a Biologist?

Biology is the science of organisms, or living things. Organisms include both plants and animals. Biologists are scientists who study organisms. They work in the field of life science.

The first biologists studied living organisms they could see with their eyes alone. They kept track of what they learned. These biologists noted the kinds of plants people could eat and which plants made people sick. They saw that some animals laid eggs, while others gave birth to live young. Biologists also studied how **habitat** affects living things, including people.

Biologists started to explain organisms to people. They showed what conditions plants and animals need to grow. They discovered why food spoils. Today, biologists help identify living organisms that are so small that a **microscope** is needed to see them.

More than **2.6 million** Americans have jobs related to biology.

About **27 percent** of people in biology-related careers are doctors, nurses, teachers, or college professors.

The **medical field** is the **#1** employer of biologists.

Biologists who work in wetlands often gather water samples. Studying the samples helps them understand the conditions needed to support a variety of plants and animals.

A STEM Job

Biologists work in the field of STEM. STEM stands for Science, Technology, Engineering, and Mathematics, or math. STEM is a developing field. Jobs in STEM change as new tools and techniques are created.

Biologists use their STEM training to understand living things. Most biologists have a focus, or specialty. Microbiologists study tiny organisms, such as germs. Zoologists are biologists who study animals.

Where Biologists Work

Biologists work for governments and private businesses. They can be found on farms and in forests, as well as in hospitals and classrooms. Some do **experiments** in research centers. Most of the United States' biology jobs are located in five states.

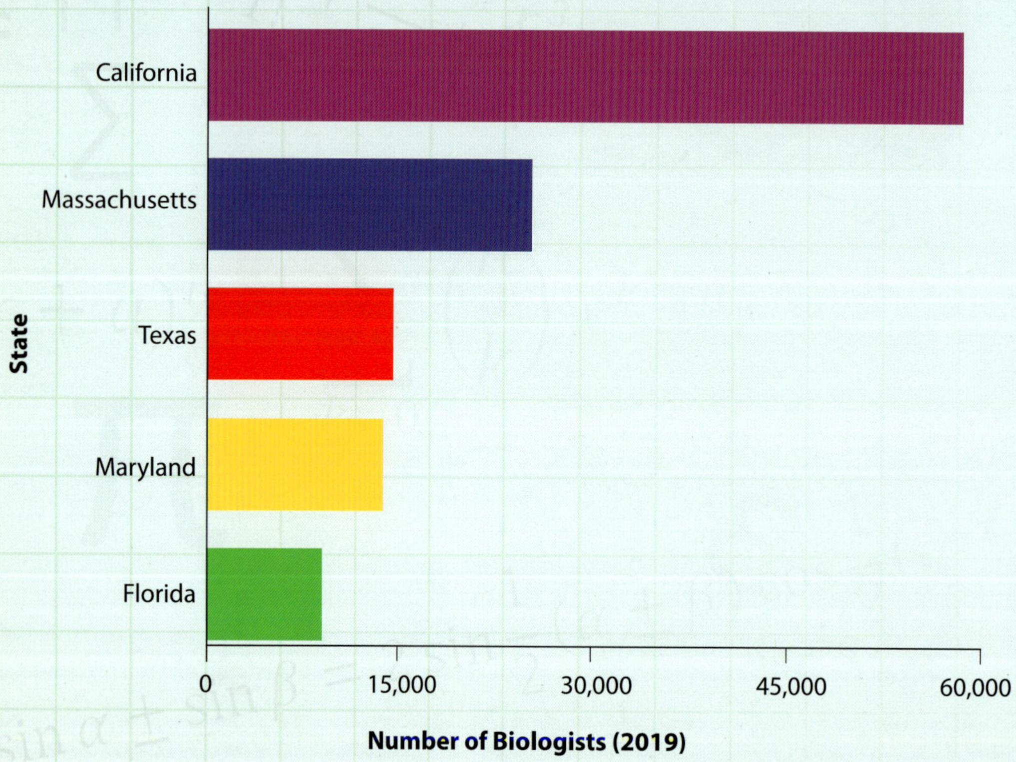

Biologists rely on all STEM fields to do their work. Engineers design biology tools, such as microscopes and scales. Biologists use scales to weigh the organisms they study. Math helps biologists take measurements. It allows them to track the weight, height, and population of their subjects. Biologists also work with technology, such as computers. These machines help biologists keep track of their research. Computers can make quick math calculations as well.

Biologists working in the medical field rely on technology to run tests for them. Technology allows the biologists to advance their study of diseases such as cancer.

STEM

U.S. biologist Judith Ramaley created the STEM **acronym** in **2001**.

Approximately **8.6 million** Americans work in STEM jobs.

STEM jobs in the United States have increased by **79 percent** since **1990**.

By **2028**, the number of STEM jobs in the United States is expected to increase by **8.8 percent**.

Laboratories

Many biologists work in science laboratories, or labs. These are rooms or buildings where biologists study **specimens**. Many labs are located in research centers.

Labs are very organized work spaces. Tools are stored in cupboards and drawers. Specimens may be stored in refrigerators. Labs have separate work areas for each biologist or research team. These workspaces are well lit. Tidy, bright work areas keep samples from getting mixed up.

Laboratories in the United States

The United States has some of the world's largest biology labs. These are very secure places. The samples inside are protected from outside **contamination**. Visitors often need permission to enter.

Natural Science and Engineering Research Laboratory
Dallas, Texas

Salk Institute for Biological Studies
San Diego, California

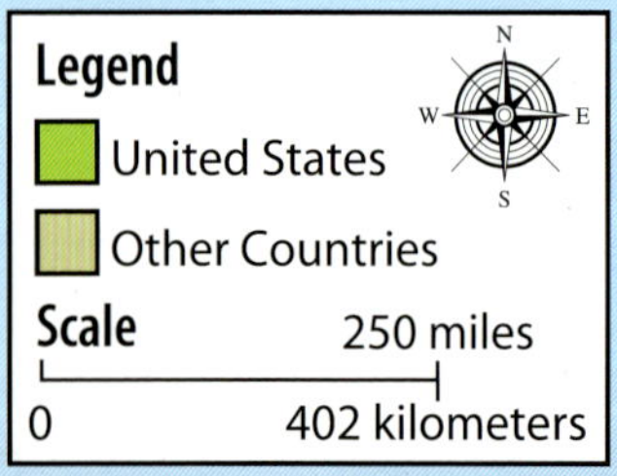

Different kinds of biologists work in different kinds of labs. Every hospital has a biology lab. Biologists in hospital labs study specimens from people. They look for germs that cause illness. Some hospital labs specialize in research. Biologists in these labs may focus on the study of human diseases, such as cancer.

Most research labs are owned by hospitals or colleges. Others are owned by private companies. Private research biologists invent new products. These products may kill weeds or help plants grow. Other inventions can benefit animal health.

Oak Ridge National Laboratory
Oak Ridge, Tennessee

Johns Hopkins University
Baltimore, Maryland

Wildlife biologists work to maintain and conserve animal populations. Field work is a key part of their job.

All in a Day's Work

Biologists can focus their attention on specific areas of study, all within the field of biology. One biologist may study how to make plants grow in dry conditions. Another biologist may investigate the decreasing deer population in a national park. A forest conservation biologist may plan experiments to determine why some trees burn faster than others. Some biologists advise governments on how to write laws that protect living things.

A biologist's day-to-day work depends on the job. Plant biologists may spend their time collecting and studying specimens. A biologist who works for a city may write a report about weeds in public spaces. Some biologists work in zoos or science centers, where they share their knowledge with visitors on a daily basis. Other biologists teach at colleges or universities.

Sample Daily Schedule

Working in a hospital can be very fast-paced. Biologists are responsible for supervising lab staff, assessing test results, and conferring with doctors about the best treatment plans for patients. They may also be required to address health issues with the public.

8:00 AM

The microbiologist arrives at the hospital lab. She checks her emails and reads reports from lab tests done during the night. She makes a list of items that need to be addressed.

10:00 AM

The microbiologist takes a call from a doctor. They talk about a patient's test results. One test shows a rare **pathogen**. The microbiologist recommends an **antibiotic** for the patient.

11:00 AM

The microbiologist meets with the team members responsible for **sterilizing** surgical instruments. She explains and demonstrates a new sterilization process.

1:00 PM

The microbiologist meets a doctor outside a hospital room. The patient in the room may have a **contagious** disease. The microbiologist will take a blood test. To enter the room, she and the doctor put on protective suits.

3:00 PM

The microbiologist studies the blood test of the patient with the unknown illness. She determines that the illness is not contagious. She calls the doctor. They agree that the patient's family can visit.

4:30 PM

The microbiologist attends a news conference to talk about an outbreak of measles. She answers questions about how the disease spreads.

Using the Scientific Method

Scientists use the scientific method to solve problems. The scientific method is a series of steps. It begins with a question scientists want to answer. First, the scientists find out if someone else has asked the same question. If so, they review that scientist's results and gather information for their work. Next, they make a hypothesis. This is what they think the answer to their question will be. The scientists then test the hypothesis with an experiment. After the experiment, they form a conclusion. This means they study the results and decide if the question was answered. Finally, the scientists share their results with the public and other scientists.

1. Ask a Question

How does refrigeration affect food decay?

2. Construct a Hypothesis

Rotten food can cause illness. Mold is one form of food decay. Food decays faster in warmer temperatures. This supports the hypothesis that refrigeration slows food decay.

3. Test with an Experiment

Take three slices of bread from the same loaf. Place each in a plastic bag. Place one bag in the fridge. Put one in a sunny spot. Put one in a drawer.
Observe all three for one week.

4. Did the Test Work?

The bread in the warmest spot grew mold first. Next, the slice in the drawer grew mold. The refrigerated bread did not grow mold.

5. Draw Conclusions

Mold grows faster in heat. Cooler temperatures slow down mold growth. This experiment showed that refrigeration slows down food decay.

Tools of the Trade

Tools help biologists get a better look at living things. Some tools make objects look bigger. Others hold objects in place. Biologists also use tools to take specimens apart.

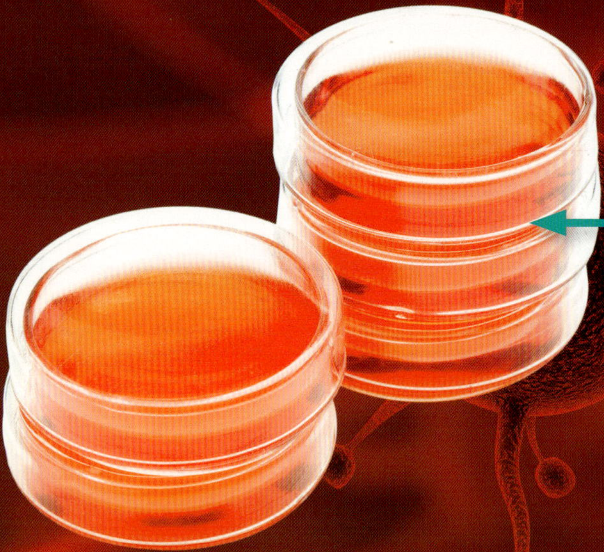

Petri Dish

Petri dishes are shallow dishes made of glass or plastic. They are used to grow specimens. The specimens may be germs, microscopic plants, or animals. Biologists grow these specimens for study.

Centrifuge

A centrifuge is a machine that is used to separate a liquid specimen into its different parts. The machine does this by spinning the liquid very fast. The specimens are usually in test tubes. When the tubes spin, the force separates the substances in the liquid by their **density**.

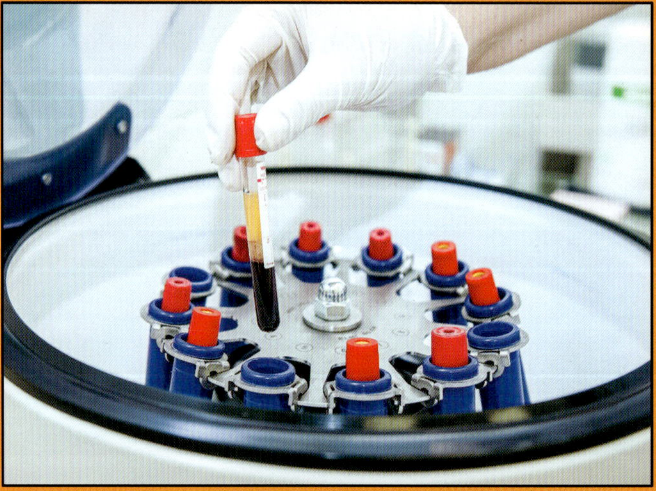

Forceps and Scalpels

Some tools let biologists study samples without touching them. This prevents biologists from contaminating a specimen. Forceps are like tweezers. They are used to pick up samples. Forceps also help biologists separate samples into different parts. Scalpels are sharp-bladed tools. They cut samples into pieces.

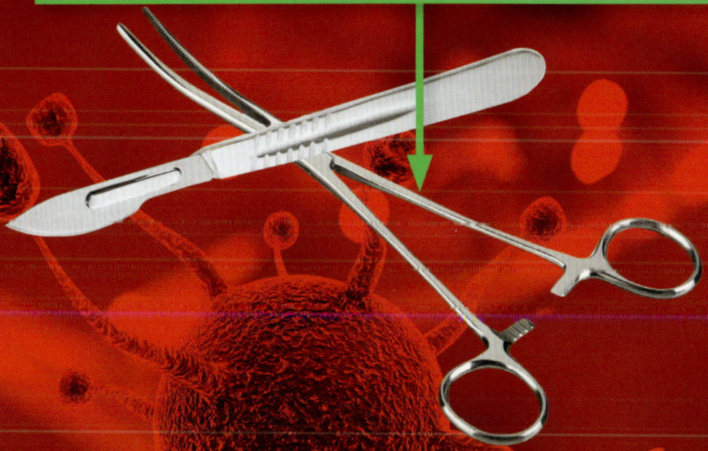

Dyes and Indicators

Dyes and indicators help biologists understand what they are looking at. Dyes make it easier to study a sample. Chemicals in the dyes highlight the parts of a sample that need to be studied. Indicators tell biologists what a specimen is made of. Litmus paper is an indicator. It shows if a sample is high in acid.

A Closer Look

Early biologists did not have the tools of today. This limited their ability to examine specimens up close. Today, biologists use microscopes to look at specimens in detail. Microscopes have changed a great deal over time.

Then

The microscope was invented in about 1590. It used lenses and light to make objects look three to nine times larger. Dutch scientist Antonie van Leeuwenhoek invented a new microscope in the 1670s. It magnified items up to 270 times their actual size, allowing biologists to see blood cells and germs up close.

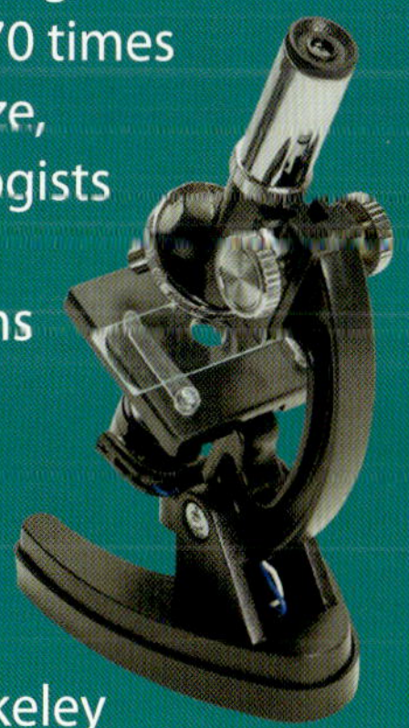

Now

Lawrence Berkeley National Laboratory has one of the most powerful microscopes in the United States. It is in California. The microscope uses **electrons** to magnify objects. It allows biologists to see items half the width of a hydrogen atom. This is half a ten-billionth of a meter.

The Biologist's Role

Biologists help people understand life on Earth. They explain how all living things are connected, showing how organisms use each other for shelter, for protection, and as a food source. Biologists teach people what living things need to be healthy. They explain why plants and animals need clean air and water. They know how **climate** affects habitat and are able to describe how a hot summer can hurt certain plants and animals.

Underwater studies help marine biologists determine ways to stop coral bleaching. Caused mainly by increased water temperatures, this condition causes coral to lose its color and die.

Today's biologists study plant and animal diseases. These diseases include those that affect people. Biologists use tools to help them understand how disease spreads. This helps them gather information and develop treatments. Biologists also use technology to study **ecological** change and the impact it has on different organisms. They may research the effects of pollution on a rainforest, the impact drilling for oil has on local wildlife, or how a growing human population is affecting both plants and animals.

Biology Breakthroughs

Biologists helped develop two of the world's most important inventions. **Vaccines** and antibiotics make some diseases less deadly. These products changed human history, allowing people to live longer and be healthier.

The **first vaccine** was developed in 1796 to treat a disease called smallpox.

The **first antibiotic**, called penicillin, was discovered in 1928. Since then, it has saved about 200 million lives.

Worldwide, vaccines prevent up to **3 million** deaths a year.

Becoming a Biologist

People who want to be biologists like asking questions. They are curious about the living organisms they see. These people wonder why apple slices turn brown. They notice that some birds eat worms, while others eat seeds. Future biologists wonder why their friends sneeze and why people get colds. Biologists-to-be participate in science fairs with projects that explore the nature of plants and animals. Potential biologists like to visit the library and often take home books about how to do experiments. They watch shows about animals in their spare time.

In high school, tomorrow's biologists take biology classes. They study chemistry. This science helps them understand what living things are made of. These students do their math homework. They visit zoos and science museums. Future biologists read books about biology and biologists.

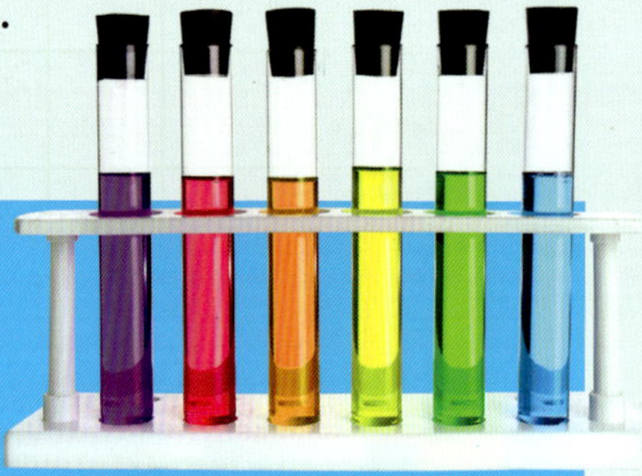

Biologist Salaries

Biologists in the United States make an average of $71,374 a year. Their annual salary depends on their field.

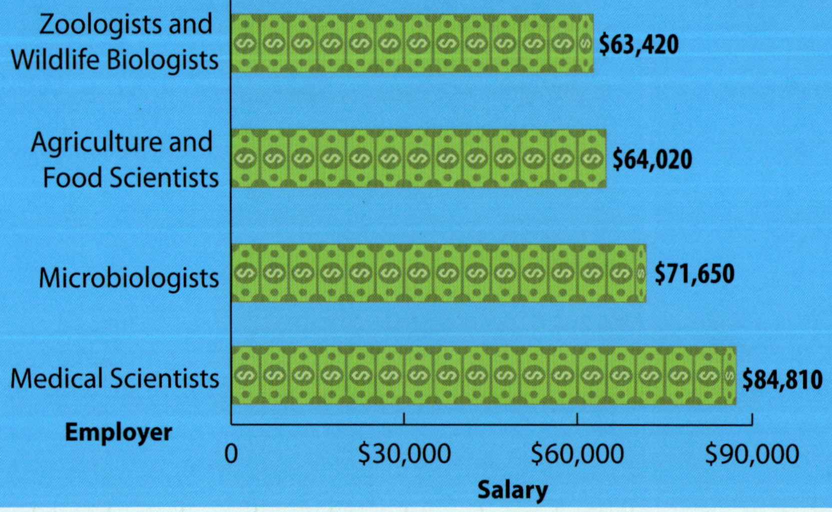

People who become biologists usually show an early interest in how organisms, whether plants or animals, function and evolve.

Is This Career For You?

Most biologists have at least one college degree. After college, they spend a great deal of time studying organisms, mostly in labs. However, some biologists also do field work. Some travel to forests to collect plants. Others spend time in another country, researching one of the animals there. If this type of work interests you, a career in biology might be a possibility.

✓ Training

Biology training begins at college. Students learn about organisms and study subjects such as ecology. These students work to hone their research skills. They write essays to show their teachers what they are learning. In lab classes, they learn how to use biology tools.

✓ Education

Most biologists have a **bachelor's degree**. This takes at least four years to complete. Some biologists do **post-graduate studies**. This takes four to six years. Biologists with the highest level of education do research. Many work in medical science.

✓ Application

Search for job postings online or in newspapers. Governments, private companies, and colleges all hire biologists. Look for jobs in the states where you want to live. Find jobs that match your education. Meet application deadlines, and include references. Employers will call references to ask about your education and work habits.

Career Connections

Plan your biology career with this activity. Follow the instructions in the steps below to complete the process of becoming a biologist.

A Talk to biologists about where they work. Visit science museums. Go to wildlife parks. Attend career days at labs. Ask working biologists where they went to college.

B Decide if you want to do this kind of work. Are you fascinated by living things? Do you like doing experiments?

C Think about the skills biologists need. Biologists are good observers. They ask questions. They learn by seeing and doing. Biologists test their ideas.

D Colleges invite future students to educational fairs. Attend a fair at a college that teaches biology. Ask what high school classes will prepare you for college.

1. Look for ways to get work experience. Join a biology club. Volunteer at a science center. Offer to help professors do research.

2. Attend career fairs in your city. Visit with companies that hire biologists. Find out where they post job information. Ask for career advice.

3. Make a list of job websites. Watch those sites for biology jobs. Look for jobs that match your training. Apply for jobs.

4. Prepare for every job interview. Find the company's website. Learn what it does. Practice answering questions you might be asked. Prepare to talk about your education and work experience.

Quiz

1. What are the tweezer-like tools that are used to pick up pieces of a biology sample?

2. In which U.S. state do most biologists work?

3. What is the name of the first antibiotic?

4. Who created the acronym STEM?

5. What is the average salary of a biologist in the United States?

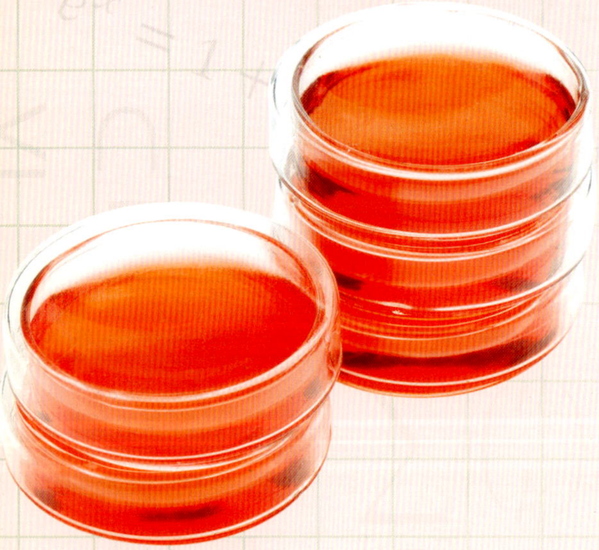

6. The microscope invented by Antonie van Leeuwenhoek magnified items to how many times their actual size?

7. By what percentage have STEM jobs in the United States increased since 1990?

8. Worldwide, how many deaths do vaccines prevent every year?

9. How many Americans hold biology-related jobs?

10. What is the name of the machine biologists use to separate a liquid specimen into its different parts?

Answers

1. Forceps
2. California
3. Penicillin
4. U.S. biologist Judith Ramaley
5. $71,374
6. 270
7. 79 percent
8. Up to 3 million
9. More than 2.6 million
10. Centrifuge

Key Words

antibiotic: a drug that kills or slows the growth of certain germs

bachelor's degree: the award earned when the first level of a college program is finished

climate: the average weather conditions of a region over a period of time

contagious: capable of being spread from one organism to another

contamination: the act of infecting or soiling by contact

density: a measurement that compares the amount of matter an object has to its volume

ecological: related to the science of living organisms and their environment

electrons: the smallest of the particles that make up an atom

experiments: tests performed to discover or prove something

habitat: the place where an animal or plant usually lives

microscope: a machine that magnifies objects

pathogen: a germ that causes disease

post-graduate studies: higher levels of college programs

specimens: samples or examples of something to be studied

sterilizing: making something completely clean and free from bacteria

vaccines: substances that protect the body from disease

Index

Published by AV2
14 Penn Plaza 9th Floor
New York, NY 10122
Website: www.av2books.com

Library of Congress Cataloging-in-Publication Data

Names: Gregory, Joy, author.
Title: Biologist / Joy Gregory.
Description: New York, NY : AV2, [2021] | Series: STEM careers | Includes index. | Audience: Ages 9-12 | Audience: Grades 4-6 |
Identifiers: LCCN 2019042837 (print) | LCCN 2019042838 (ebook) | ISBN 9781791116965 (library binding) | ISBN 9781791116972 (paperback) | ISBN 9781791116989 | ISBN 9781791116996
Subjects: LCSH: Biologists--Vocational guidance--Juvenile literature.
Classification: LCC QH49 .G74 2021 (print) | LCC QH49 (ebook) | DDC 570.92 [B]--dc23
LC record available at https://lccn.loc.gov/2019042837
LC ebook record available at https://lccn.loc.gov/2019042838

Printed in Guangzhou, China
1 2 3 4 5 6 7 8 9 0 24 23 22 21 20

052020
101119

Project Coordinator: Heather Kissock
Designer: Ana María Vidal

Every reasonable effort has been made to trace ownership and to obtain permission to reprint copyright material. The publishers would be pleased to have any errors or omissions brought to their attention so that they may be corrected in subsequent printings.

The publisher acknowledges Getty Images, Alamy, Shutterstock, iStock, and Wikimedia Commons as its primary image suppliers for this title.